Those Who Love

THOSE WHO LOVE

LOVE POEMS BY SARA TEASDALE
EDITED BY ARTHUR WORTMAN
ILLUSTRATED BY BILL GREER

HALLMARK EDITIONS

SARA TEASDALE'S POETRY includes some of the most beautiful love poems ever written by a woman. Love, as Miss Teasdale wrote of it, is something felt and cherished by sensitive people of all eras. Her poems are simple, lyrical, poignant outpourings of the heart. She writes of loneliness and fulfillment, longing and joy, of love's ecstasy and pain, and always of beauty as she sees it in music, the sea, the stars, the face of the beloved.

Miss Teasdale was born in St. Louis in 1884 in an atmosphere and a time highly stimulating to creative talent. Her first book, *Sonnets to Duse,* was published in 1907 when she was in her early twenties. In 1918, *Love Songs* was awarded the Columbia-Poetry Society of America Prize, forerunner of the Pulitzer Prize for poetry. She published eight volumes of poetry, the last of which, *Strange Victory,* appeared in 1933.

In 1914, Miss Teasdale married Ernst Filsinger, a St. Louis businessman. The early years of their marriage were happy ones, spent in New York City, which she loved and where she had many friends. However, long periods of separation because of her husband's increased business interests abroad led to divergence in their ways of life, and they were divorced in 1929.

Miss Teasdale's later years were saddened by her divorce, by the death of her close friend Vachel Lindsay, by increasing ill health and by the loneliness

which illness and her need for solitude brought.
Physical frailty limited her activities all her life, but
her poetry continued to deepen in meaning and to
grow in beauty.

Many of her poems have been set to music.
Individual poems have been translated into a number
of languages including Danish, French and Spanish,
and there are German and Japanese editions of
certain selected poems.

She was a severe critic of her own work and
indicated those poems which she felt should be
included in a collected edition. Four years after her
death, *The Collected Poems of Sara Teasdale* was
published by The Macmillan Company. The selections
in this edition come from that book.

Sara Teasdale: A Biography, by Margaret Haley
Carpenter, gives a warm and accurate picture of her
life and of the forces that moved her: beauty, love
and friendship, her own "singing voice," and her
rebellion against death.

Certainly Sara Teasdale has found the spiritual
immortality for which she longed; she lives today in
her exquisite poetry. As she wrote in "Moon Ending":

> *Moon, worn thin to the width of a quill,*
> *In the dawn clouds flying,*
> *How good to go, light into light, and still*
> *Giving light, dying.*

—Margaret Conklin

THE POEMS

THOSE WHO LOVE

Those who love the most,
Do not talk of their love,
Francesca, Guinevere,
Deirdre, Iseult, Heloise,
In the fragrant gardens of heaven
Are silent, or speak if at all
Of fragile, inconsequent things.

And a woman I used to know
Who loved one man from her youth,
Against the strength of the fates
Fighting in somber pride,
Never spoke of this thing,
But hearing his name by chance,
A light would pass over her face.

7

HOUSE OF DREAMS

You took my empty dreams
  And filled them every one
With tenderness and nobleness,
  April and the sun.

The old empty dreams
  Where my thoughts would throng
Are far too full of happiness
  To even hold a song.

Oh, the empty dreams were dim
  And the empty dreams were wide,
They were sweet and shadowy houses
  Where my thoughts could hide.

But you took my dreams away
  And you made them all come true—
My thoughts have no place now to play,
  And nothing now to do.

SHE WHO COULD BIND YOU

She who could bind you
  Could bind fire to a wall;
She who could hold you
  Could hold a waterfall;
She who could keep you
  Could keep the wind from blowing
On a warm spring night
  With a low moon glowing.

THE KISS

I hoped that he would love me,
  And he has kissed my mouth,
But I am like a stricken bird
  That cannot reach the south.

For though I know he loves me,
  To-night my heart is sad;
His kiss was not so wonderful
  As all the dreams I had.

I WOULD LIVE IN YOUR LOVE

I would live in your love as the
    sea-grasses live in the sea,
Borne up by each wave as it passes,
    drawn down by each wave that recedes;
I would empty my soul of the dreams
    that have gathered in me,
I would beat with your heart as it beats,
    I would follow your soul as it leads.

SONG

You bound strong sandals on my feet,
    You gave me bread and wine,
And sent me under sun and stars,
    For all the world was mine.

Oh, take the sandals off my feet,
    You know not what you do;
For all my world is in your arms,
    My sun and stars are you.

THE WISE WOMAN

She must be rich who can forego
    An hour so jewelled with delight,
She must have treasuries of joy
    That she can draw on day and night,
She must be very sure of heaven—
    Or is it only that she feels
How much more safe it is to lack
    A thing that time so often steals.

LESS THAN THE CLOUD TO THE WIND

Less than the cloud to the wind,
    Less than the foam to the sea,
Less than the rose to the storm
    Am I to thee.

More than the star to the night,
    More than the rain to the tree,
More than heaven to earth
    Art thou to me.

DEW

I dream that he is mine,
   I dream that he is true,
And all his words I keep
   As rose-leaves hold the dew.

O little thirsty rose,
   O little heart beware,
Lest you should hope to hold
   A hundred roses' share.

AGE

Brooks sing in the spring
   And in summer cease;
I who sang in my youth
   Now hold my peace;
Youth is a noisy stream
   Chattering over the ground,
But the sad wisdom of age
   Wells up without sound.

FAULTS

They came to tell your faults to me,
They named them over one by one;
I laughed aloud when they were done,
I knew them all so well before,—
Oh, they were blind, too blind to see
Your faults had made me love you more.

LET IT BE YOU

Let it be you who lean above me
      On my last day,
Let it be you who shut my eyelids
      Forever and aye.

Say a "Good-night" as you have said it
      All of these years,
With the old look, with the old whisper
      And without tears.

You will know then all that in silence
      You always knew,
Though I have loved, I loved no other
      As I love you.

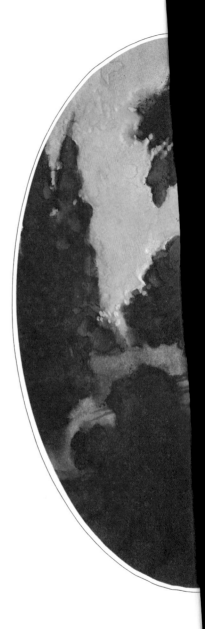

DEW

I dream that he is mine,
    I dream that he is true,
And all his words I keep
    As rose-leaves hold the dew.

O little thirsty rose,
    O little heart beware,
Lest you should hope to hold
    A hundred roses' share.

AGE

Brooks sing in the spring
    And in summer cease;
I who sang in my youth
    Now hold my peace;
Youth is a noisy stream
    Chattering over the ground,
But the sad wisdom of age
    Wells up without sound.

FAULTS

They came to tell your faults to me,
They named them over one by one;
I laughed aloud when they were done,
I knew them all so well before,—
Oh, they were blind, too blind to see
Your faults had made me love you more.

LET IT BE YOU

Let it be you who lean above me
    On my last day,
Let it be you who shut my eyelids
    Forever and aye.

Say a "Good-night" as you have said it
    All of these years,
With the old look, with the old whisper
    And without tears.

You will know then all that in silence
    You always knew,
Though I have loved, I loved no other
    As I love you.

ADVICE TO A GIRL

No one worth possessing
Can be quite possessed;
Lay that on your heart,
My young angry dear;
This truth, this hard and precious stone,
Lay it on your hot cheek,
Let it hide your tear.
Hold it like a crystal
When you are alone
And gaze in the depths of the icy stone.
Long, look long and you will be blessed:
No one worth possessing
Can be quite possessed.

SPRING NIGHT

The park is filled with night and fog,
　　The veils are drawn about the world,
The drowsy lights along the paths
　　Are dim and pearled.

Gold and gleaming the empty streets,
　　Gold and gleaming the misty lake,
The mirrored lights like sunken swords,
　　Glimmer and shake.

Oh, is it not enough to be
Here with this beauty over me?
My throat should ache with praise, and I
Should kneel in joy beneath the sky.
O, beauty are you not enough?
Why am I crying after love,
With youth, a singing voice and eyes
To take earth's wonder with surprise?
Why have I put off my pride,
Why am I unsatisfied,—
I for whom the pensive night
Binds her cloudy hair with light,—
I, for whom all beauty burns
Like incense in a million urns?
O, beauty, are you not enough?
Why am I crying after love?

CHILD, CHILD

Child, child, love while you can
The voice and the eyes and the soul of a man;
Never fear though it break your heart—
Out of the wound new joy will start;
Only love proudly and gladly and well,
Though love be heaven or love be hell.

Child, child, love while you may,
For life is short as a happy day;
Never fear the thing you feel—
Only by love is life made real;
Love, for the deadly sins are seven,
Only through love will you enter heaven.

GIFTS

I gave my first love laughter,
   I gave my second tears,
I gave my third love silence
   Through all the years.

My first love gave me singing,
   My second eyes to see,
But oh, it was my third love
   Who gave my soul to me.

WILD ASTERS

In the spring I asked the daisies
   If his words were true,
And the clever little daisies
   Always knew.

Now the fields are brown and barren,
   Bitter autumn blows,
And of all the stupid asters
   Not one knows.

SPRING RAIN

I thought I had forgotten,
　　But it all came back again
To-night with the first spring thunder
　　In a rush of rain.

I remembered a darkened doorway
　　Where we stood while the storm swept by,
Thunder gripping the earth
　　And lightning scrawled on the sky.

The passing motor busses swayed,
　　For the street was a river of rain,
Lashed into little golden waves
　　In the lamp light's stain.

With the wild spring rain and thunder
　　My heart was wild and gay;
Your eyes said more to me that night
　　Than your lips would ever say. . . .

I thought I had forgotten,
　　But it all came back again
To-night with the first spring thunder
　　In a rush of rain.

BECAUSE

Oh, because you never tried
To bow my will or break my pride,
And nothing of the cave-man made
You want to keep me half afraid,
Nor ever with a conquering air
You thought to draw me unaware—
Take me, for I love you more
Than I ever loved before.

And since the body's maidenhood
Alone were neither rare nor good
Unless with it I gave to you
A spirit still untrammeled, too,
Take my dreams and take my mind
That were masterless as wind;
And "Master!" I shall say to you
Since you never asked me to.

THERE WILL BE STARS

There will be stars over the place forever;
    Though the house we loved and the street
        we loved are lost,
Every time the earth circles her orbit
    On the night the autumn equinox is crossed,
Two stars we knew, poised on the peak of midnight
    Will reach their zenith; stillness will be deep;
There will be stars over the place forever,
    There will be stars forever, while we sleep.

THE WIND

A wind is blowing over my soul,
    I hear it cry the whole night through—
Is there no peace for me on earth
    Except with you?

Alas, the wind has made me wise,
    Over my naked soul it blew,—
There is no peace for me on earth
    Even with you.

I SHALL NOT CARE

When I am dead and over me bright April
   Shakes out her rain-drenched hair,
Tho' you should lean above me broken-hearted,
   I shall not care.

I shall have peace, as leafy trees are peaceful
   When rain bends down the bough,
And I shall be more silent and cold-hearted
   Than you are now.

NIGHT SONG AT AMALFI

I asked the heaven of stars
   What I should give my love—
It answered me with silence,
   Silence above.

I asked the darkened sea
   Down where the fishers go—
It answered me with silence,
   Silence below.

Oh, I could give him weeping,
   Or I could give him song—
But how can I give silence
   My whole life long?

THE GIFT

What can I give you, my lord, my lover,
You who have given the world to me,
Showed me the light and the joy that cover
The wild sweet earth and the restless sea?

All that I have are gifts of your giving—
If I gave them again, you would find them old,
And your soul would weary of always living
Before the mirror my life would hold.

What shall I give you, my lord, my lover?
The gift that breaks the heart in me:
I bid you awake at dawn and discover
I have gone my way and left you free.

DESERT POOLS

I love too much; I am a river
  Surging with spring that seeks the sea,
I am too generous a giver,
  Love will not stoop to drink of me.

His feet will turn to desert places
  Shadowless, reft of rain and dew,
Where stars stare down with sharpened faces
  From heavens pitilessly blue.

And there at midnight sick with faring,
  He will stoop down in his desire
To slake the thirst grown past all bearing
  In stagnant water keen as fire.

IN A RESTAURANT

The darkened street was muffled with the snow,
    The falling flakes had made your shoulders white,
    And when we found a shelter from the night
Its glamor fell upon us like a blow.
The clash of dishes and the viol and bow
    Mingled beneath the fever of the light.
    The heat was full of savors, and the bright
Laughter of women lured the wine to flow.
A little child ate nothing while she sat
    Watching a woman at a table there
Lean to a kiss beneath a drooping hat.
        The hour went by, we rose and turned to go,
        The somber street received us from the glare,
        And once more on your shoulders fell the snow.

I KNOW THE STARS

I know the stars by their names,
  Aldebaran, Altair,
And I know the path they take
  Up heaven's broad blue stair.

I know the secrets of men
  By the look of their eyes,
Their gray thoughts, their strange thoughts
  Have made me sad and wise.

But your eyes are dark to me
  Though they seem to call and call—
I cannot tell if you love me
  Or do not love me at all.

I know many things,
  But the years come and go,
I shall die not knowing
  The thing I long to know.

APPRAISAL

Never think she loves him wholly,
Never believe her love is blind,
All his faults are locked securely
In a closet of her mind;
All his indecisions folded
Like old flags that time has faded,
Limp and streaked with rain,
And his cautiousness like garments
Frayed and thin, with many a stain—
Let them be, oh let them be,
There is treasure to outweigh them,
His proud will that sharply stirred,
Climbs as surely as the tide,
Senses strained too taut to sleep,
Gentleness to beast and bird,
Humor flickering hushed and wide
As the moon on moving water,
And a tenderness too deep
To be gathered in a word.

SUMMER NIGHT, RIVERSIDE

In the wild soft summer darkness
How many and many a night we two together
Sat in the park and watched the Hudson
Wearing her lights like golden spangles
Glinting on black satin.
The rail along the curving pathway
Was low in a happy place to let us cross,
And down the hill a tree that dripped with bloom
Sheltered us,
While your kisses and the flowers,
Falling, falling,
Tangled my hair. . . .

The frail white stars moved slowly over the sky.

And now, far off
In the fragrant darkness
The tree is tremulous again with bloom
For June comes back.

To-night what girl
Dreamily before her mirror shakes from her hair
This year's blossoms, clinging in its coils?

NIGHT SONG AT AMALFI

I asked the heaven of stars
   What I should give my love—
It answered me with silence,
   Silence above.

I asked the darkened sea
   Down where the fishers go—
It answered me with silence,
   Silence below.

Oh, I could give him weeping,
   Or I could give him song—
But how can I give silence
   My whole life long?

BECAUSE

Oh, because you never tried
To bow my will or break my pride,
And nothing of the cave-man made
You want to keep me half afraid,
Nor ever with a conquering air
You thought to draw me unaware—
Take me, for I love you more
Than I ever loved before.

And since the body's maidenhood
Alone were neither rare nor good
Unless with it I gave to you
A spirit still untrammeled, too,
Take my dreams and take my mind
That were masterless as wind;
And "Master!" I shall say to you
Since you never asked me to.

THERE WILL BE STARS

There will be stars over the place forever;
    Though the house we loved and the street
      we loved are lost,
Every time the earth circles her orbit
    On the night the autumn equinox is crossed,
Two stars we knew, poised on the peak of midnight
    Will reach their zenith; stillness will be deep;
There will be stars over the place forever,
    There will be stars forever, while we sleep.

THE WIND

A wind is blowing over my soul,
    I hear it cry the whole night through—
Is there no peace for me on earth
    Except with you?

Alas, the wind has made me wise,
    Over my naked soul it blew,—
There is no peace for me on earth
    Even with you.

I SHALL NOT CARE

When I am dead and over me bright April
    Shakes out her rain-drenched hair,
Tho' you should lean above me broken-hearted,
    I shall not care.

I shall have peace, as leafy trees are peaceful
    When rain bends down the bough,
And I shall be more silent and cold-hearted
    Than you are now.

PEACE

Peace flows into me
    As the tide to the pool by the shore;
    It is mine forevermore,
It ebbs not back like the sea.

I am the pool of blue
    That worships the vivid sky;
    My hopes were heaven-high,
They are all fulfilled in you.

I am the pool of gold
    When sunset burns and dies,—
    You are my deepening skies,
Give me your stars to hold.

THE NET

I made you many and many a song,
　　Yet never one told all you are—
It was as though a net of words
　　Were flung to catch a star;

It was as though I curved my hand
　　And dipped sea-water eagerly,
Only to find it lost the blue
　　Dark splendor of the sea.

THE STORM

I thought of you when I was wakened
　　By a wind that made me glad and afraid
Of the rushing, pouring sound of the sea
　　That the great trees made.

One thought in my mind went over and over
　　While the darkness shook and the leaves
　　　　were thinned—
I thought it was you who had come to find me,
　　You were the wind.

THE FLIGHT

We are two eagles
Flying together
Under the heavens,
Over the mountains,
Stretched on the wind.
Sunlight heartens us,
Blind snow baffles us,
Clouds wheel after us
Ravelled and thinned.

We are like eagles,
But when Death harries us,
Human and humbled
When one of us goes,
Let the other follow,
Let the flight be ended,
Let the fire blacken,
Let the book close.

NIGHT

Stars over snow
    And in the west a planet
Swinging below a star—
    Look for a lovely thing and you will find it,
It is not far—
    It never will be far.

JEWELS

If I should see your eyes again,
    I know how far their look would go—
Back to a morning in the park
    With sapphire shadows on the snow.

Or back to oak trees in the spring
    When you unloosed my hair and kissed
The head that lay against your knees
    In the leaf shadow's amethyst.

And still another shining place
    We would remember—how the dun
Wild mountain held us on its crest
    One diamond morning white with sun.

But I will turn my eyes from you
    As women turn to put away
The jewels they have worn at night
    And cannot wear in sober day.

BARTER

Life has loveliness to sell,
    All beautiful and splendid things,
Blue waves whitened on a cliff,
    Soaring fire that sways and sings,
And children's faces looking up
Holding wonder like a cup.

Life has loveliness to sell,
    Music like a curve of gold,
Scent of pine trees in the rain,
    Eyes that love you, arms that hold,
And for your spirit's still delight,
Holy thoughts that star the night.

Spend all you have for loveliness,
    Buy it and never count the cost;
For one white singing hour of peace
    Count many a year of strife well lost,
And for a breath of ecstasy
Give all you have been, or could be.

THE SOLITARY

My heart has grown rich with the passing of years,
  I have less need now than when I was young
To share myself with every comer
  Or shape my thoughts into words with my tongue.

It is one to me that they come or go
  If I have myself and the drive of my will,
And strength to climb on a summer night
  And watch the stars swarm over the hill.

Let them think I love them more than I do,
  Let them think I care, though I go alone;
If it lifts their pride, what is it to me
  Who am self-complete as a flower or a stone.

PRIMAVERA MIA

As kings, seeing their lives about to pass,
Take off the heavy ermine and the crown,
So had the trees that autumn-time laid down
Their golden garments on the dying grass,
When I, who watched the seasons in the glass
Of my own thoughts, saw all the autumn's brown
Leap into life and wear a sunny gown
Of leafage fresh as happy April has.
Great spring came singing upward from the south;
For in my heart, far carried on the wind,
Your words like winged seeds took root and grew,
And all the world caught music from your mouth;
I saw the light as one who had been blind,
And knew my sun and song and spring were you.

THE LOOK

Strephon kissed me in the spring,
   Robin in the fall,
But Colin only looked at me
   And never kissed at all.

Strephon's kiss was lost in jest,
   Robin's lost in play,
But the kiss in Colin's eyes
   Haunts me night and day.

THE COIN

Into my heart's treasury
   I slipped a coin
That time cannot take
   Nor a thief purloin,—
Oh, better than the minting
   Of a gold-crowned king
Is the safe-kept memory
   Of a lovely thing.

DEBT

What do I owe to you
   Who loved me deep and long?
You never gave my spirit wings
   Or gave my heart a song.

But oh, to him I loved
   Who loved me not at all,
I owe the open gate
   That led thru heaven's wall.

ALCHEMY

I lift my heart as spring lifts up
   A yellow daisy to the rain;
My heart will be a lovely cup
   Altho' it holds but pain.

For I shall learn from flower and leaf
   That color every drop they hold,
To change the lifeless wine of grief
   To living gold.

MORNING SONG

A diamond of a morning
   Waked me an hour too soon;
Dawn had taken in the stars
   And left the faint white moon.

O white moon, you are lonely,
   It is the same with me,
But we have the world to roam over,
   Only the lonely are free.

THE METROPOLITAN TOWER

We walked together in the dusk
  To watch the tower grow dimly white,
And saw it lift against the sky
  Its flower of amber light.

You talked of half a hundred things,
  I kept each hurried word you said;
And when at last the hour was full,
  I saw the light turn red.

You did not know the time had come,
  You did not see the sudden flower,
Nor know that in my heart Love's birth
  Was reckoned from that hour.

ON A MARCH DAY

Here in the teeth of this triumphant wind
　　That shakes the naked shadows on the ground,
Making a key-board of the earth to strike
　　From clattering tree and hedge a separate sound,

Bear witness for me that I loved my life,
　　All things that hurt me and all things that healed,
And that I swore to it this day in March,
　　Here at the edge of this new-broken field.

You only knew me, tell them I was glad
　　For every hour since my hour of birth,
And that I ceased to fear, as once I feared,
　　The last complete reunion with the earth.

PIERROT

Pierrot stands in the garden
   Beneath a waning moon,
And on his lute he fashions
   A fragile silver tune.

Pierrot plays in the garden,
   He thinks he plays for me,
But I am quite forgotten
   Under the cherry tree.

Pierrot plays in the garden,
   And all the roses know
That Pierrot loves his music,—
   But I love Pierrot.

MAY DAY

A delicate fabric of bird song
    Floats in the air,
The smell of wet wild earth
    Is everywhere.

Red small leaves of the maple
    Are clenched like a hand,
Like girls at their first communion
    The pear trees stand.

Oh I must pass nothing by
    Without loving it much,
The raindrop try with my lips,
    The grass with my touch;

For how can I be sure
    I shall see again
The world on the first of May
    Shining after the rain?

TO JOY

Lo, I am happy, for my eyes have seen
Joy glowing here before me, face to face;
His wings were arched above me for a space,
I kissed his lips, no bitter came between.
The air is vibrant where his feet have been,
And full of song and color is his place.
His wondrous presence sheds about a grace
That lifts and hallows all that once was mean.
I may not sorrow for I saw the light,
Tho' I shall walk in valley ways for long,
I still shall hear the echo of the song,—
My life is measured by its one great height.
Joy holds more grace than pain can ever give,
And by my glimpse of joy my soul shall live.

DAY'S ENDING (*Tucson*)

Aloof as aged kings,
Wearing like them the purple,
The mountains ring the mesa
Crowned with a dusky light;
Many a time I watched
That coming-on of darkness
Till stars burned through the heavens
Intolerably bright.

It was not long I lived there
But I became a woman
Under those vehement stars,
For it was there I heard
For the first time my spirit
Forging an iron rule for me,
As though with slow cold hammers
Beating out word by word:

"Only yourself can heal you,
Only yourself can lead you,
The road is heavy going
And ends where no man knows;
Take love when love is given,
But never think to find it
A sure escape from sorrow
Or a complete repose."

52

THE BELOVED

It is enough of honor for one lifetime
  To have known you better than the rest have known,
The shadows and the colors of your voice,
  Your will, immutable and still as stone.

The shy heart, so lonely and so gay,
  The sad laughter and the pride of pride,
The tenderness, the depth of tenderness
  Rich as the earth, and wide as heaven is wide.

THE LAMP

If I can bear your love like a lamp before me,
When I go down the long steep Road of Darkness,
I shall not fear the everlasting shadows,
        Nor cry in terror.

If I can find out God, then I shall find Him,
If none can find Him, then I shall sleep soundly,
Knowing how well on earth your love sufficed me,
        A lamp in darkness.

DRIFTWOOD

My forefathers gave me
　　My spirit's shaken flame,
The shape of hands, the beat of heart,
　　The letters of my name.

But it was my lovers,
　　And not my sleeping sires,
Who gave the flame its changeful
　　And iridescent fires;

As the driftwood burning
　　Learned its jewelled blaze
From the sea's blue splendor
　　Of colored nights and days.

LOVELY CHANCE

O lovely chance, what can I do
To give my gratefulness to you?
You rise between myself and me
With a wise persistency;
I would have broken body and soul,
But by your grace, still I am whole.
Many a thing you did to save me,
Many a holy gift you gave me,
Music and friends and happy love
More than my dearest dreaming of;
And now in this wide twilight hour
With earth and heaven a dark, blue flower,
In a humble mood I bless
Your wisdom—and your waywardness.
You brought me even here, where I
Live on a hill against the sky
And look on mountains and the sea
And a thin white moon in the pepper tree.

WINTER

I shall have winter now and lessening days,
Lit by a smoky sun with slanting rays,
And after falling leaves, the first determined frost.
The colors of the world will all be lost.
So be it; the faint buzzing of the snow
Will fill the empty boughs,
And after sleet storms I shall wake to see
A glittering glassy plume of every tree.
Nothing shall tempt me from my fire-lit house.
And I shall find at night a friendly ember
And make my life of what I can remember.

CONEY ISLAND

Why did you bring me here?
The sand is white with snow,
Over the wooden domes
The winter sea-winds blow—
There is no shelter near,
   Come, let us go.

With foam of icy lace
The sea creeps up the sand,
The wind is like a hand
That strikes us in the face.
Doors that June set a-swing
Are bolted long ago;
We try them uselessly—
Alas, there cannot be
For us a second spring;
   Come, let us go.

LONGING

I am not sorry for my soul
    That it must go unsatisfied,
For it can live a thousand times,
    Eternity is deep and wide.

I am not sorry for my soul,
    But oh, my body that must go
Back to a little drift of dust
    Without the joy it longed to know.

TWO MINDS

Your mind and mine are such great lovers they
Have freed themselves from cautious human clay,
And on wild clouds of thought, naked together
They ride above us in extreme delight;
We see them, we look up with a lone envy
And watch them in their zone of crystal weather
That changes not for winter or the night.

AFTER LOVE

There is no magic any more,
    We meet as other people do,
You work no miracle for me
    Nor I for you.

You were the wind and I the sea—
    There is no splendor any more,
I have grown listless as the pool
    Beside the shore.

But tho' the pool is safe from storm
    And from the tide has found surcease,
It grows more bitter than the sea,
    For all its peace.

CLEAR EVENING

The crescent moon is large enough to linger
   A little while after the twilight goes,
This moist midsummer night the garden perfumes
   Are earth and apple, dewy pine and rose.

Over my head four new-cut stars are glinting
   And the inevitable night draws on;
I am alone, the old terror takes me,
   Evenings will come like this when I am gone;

Evenings on evenings, years on years forever—
   Be taut, my spirit, close upon and keep
The scent, the brooding chill, the gliding fire-fly,
   A poem learned before I fall asleep.

Set in Goudy light Old Style, a delicately-styled
original alphabet drawn by the American designer
Frederic W. Goudy for the Monotype in 1905.
Printed on Hallmark Eggshell Book paper.
Designed by Harald Peter.